The Secret Atheist

Michael User

Michael User

www.michaeluser.com All rights reserved.

ISBN-13: 978-0615636290
ISBN-10: 0615636292

Summary

The Secret Atheist exposes the author and everyone, on the secret disbelief that God really exists. It shows how even the most religious figures, from all walks of life and religions, don't actually believe in God and eternal justice. The proofs and the following corrective skills provide a practical, down to earth guide on how to live your life as a genuine believer. With this revelation of true belief in God, and armed with the real reasons behind the things you want and desire, your goals will be within your reach with godly support.

About the Author

Michael User is a born expatriate, and lived in four countries in Western and Eastern Europe before settling in the United States. One night, he discovered that he had secretly been an atheist most of his life and started thinking about God, and suddenly many answers appear. Mr. User is an active executive in a global American firm and lives in Danbury, Connecticut, with his wife and their cat.

*To my brother, the rock of character and principle
that is a safe haven in the stormy waters of my life*

ACKNOWLEDGMENTS

My beloved wife turned a switch inside me after I met her. I started writing poems for her, and one of our fights actually triggered this book. She deserves all the credit and, of course, has all my love.

My mother has made me who I am today, patiently forming a strong conscience in me that actually guided most of the rules in my life and in this book. If there is anything godly in my life, it's she.

My grandmother is the essence of love in all our family, the root that created us all, and the one who instilled strong ethics throughout our family. She is my strongest supporter and the origin of my "culture."

Michael User

1

HOW THIS BOOK CAME TO BE

It is true, that a little philosophy inclineth man's mind to atheism,
but depth in philosophy bringeth men's minds about to religion.
~ Francis Bacon

I am a lost person; I've been lost for some time. I'm away from my family, friends, and cultures that created me. I've been away from myself. I've chosen to be away for a long time now. No, I did not vanish, become anti-social, or let myself go. I'm still working, I still have a successful career, and I still live a good life.

But I'd been lost. I didn't know what to do. I'm sure you've felt like me at some point in your life. I had everything in control and nothing in control. My marriage was collapsing. My wife and I had gone through a separation for four months and then decided to divorce. All my plans were broken. My future in my mind was gone. I no longer had a path to follow. I didn't know what to do.

And, to put this in context, I'm away from everything I know. I had decided to relocate to the United States about a year ago and started working in the US five months after transitioning from my role in Geneva. I no longer have a plan or any sense of what I'm doing, why I'm doing it, or if I should continue doing anything at all.

I couldn't make sense of what was happening around me. And that's when it happened. One day after our divorce decision and four months after my father's death, I was alone trying to make sense of my life. Why was God punishing me? What had I done wrong?

I'm not a religious person; in fact, I don't consider myself to have a religion. I'm very close to Jewish, Christian, Muslim, and even Hinduism values due to the cultures that made me who I am. But I don't hold a religion; I have not been part of any organized religion since childhood. I do believe in one very strong thing. I was created. Whether it was through evolution or whether it was through intelligent design, I have a creator. Jesus, our Lord, Elohim, YHWH, Allah, Krishna, or any name or concept that may be in your mind, I believe in him. I'm not sure he's a he or a she or that he even needs this distinction. But I believe he created me. And I will refer to him as he in this book.

I believe he is great—the creator with a purpose. He was my anchor as I tried to make sense of it all—or so I thought, until I suddenly wondered if I really believed in God. Did I really believe the all-knowing, all-powerful, eternally just God was aware what was happening to me and to everyone in this world?

I suddenly realized, No! I thought I believed in him. In reality, I was thinking everything I did, every opportunity I had, and all my life was a series of good decisions, bad decisions, and opportunities that materialized or not. As I said, I've been lost for a long time, and to understand what I mean, I will give you a brief insight into who I am and how I came to be.

2

HOW I CAME TO BE

I am a human being, created by God through my parents. My parents consider themselves Turkish. My father's ancestors were Crimean Tatar Krymchaks. They relocated to Eskisehir in Turkey during the tough times they faced under the Soviet regime, and they became integrated to Turkish society. My mother's ancestors were Aegean Turks living close to Izmir. Both families moved to Istanbul at one point, where they met.

I was born in Germany after my family relocated while my father was working and studying for his master's degree. I was born an expat, which seemed to resonate all through my life. I was born lost, away from my own creating culture.

We lived in Germany until a time I don't remember; I was only a child, and I don't remember the Germany that we lived in. We lived in Frankfurt at a time when many immigrants from all over Europe and Turkey were still moving to Germany. As a baby who just started walking, I had a serious condition. My parents took me from hospital to hospital and doctor to doctor, trying to find out what was wrong with me. I was not eating or drinking, and anything that I consumed came out right away. I don't remember anything, but I spent almost two months in the Frankfurt university clinic. The clinic where I was actually born in, under intensive care of friendly German nurses and doctors. My condition just fixed itself, with no diagnosis whatsoever, until it reemerged years later.

After some time, we relocated back to Istanbul, where I spent my childhood. We had a lot of fights in my family, and others may think I had a terrible childhood. On the contrary, I had a great childhood! In Turkey, many well-to-do families have two homes: one for the winter and one for the summer. Families visit summer homes when children have their summer holidays. It's a joyous occasion when families transfer many things from the winter homes to the summer homes, and three-month vacations start for the children. Working parents continue to work, so summer homes close to Istanbul but still on the seaside are high in demand.

Our first summer home was in Caddebostan, Istanbul. It was on "the other side" as others called it then. Istanbul is in two continents, Europe and Asia, and the other side was Asia. This was a time when a heavily trafficked bridge connected the two parts. Since then the city has built a second one. We normally never crossed the bridge. We never needed to until we were moving to our summer home once a year! It was magical.

We packed everything up, crossed the bridge, and resettled in our home in Caddebostan. It had a nice garden around it and was only a few minutes walk to the sea, where we went everyday to swim. I remember the small local grocery store around the corner where I bought, with the little pocket money I had, very red, pacifier candy—gums that came wrapped in cartoons or pictures of cars, such as Tipitip and Turbo (I think). My only worry was which cartoon or car I would get.

One summer, my biggest passion was collecting soda caps. This was because a girl my age was collecting them also. There was no point in collecting them, as they had no value, and they were filthy and rusty. But this was something to do in an otherwise aimless summer. I was in constant competition with the girl I secretly liked. She always had more caps! I used to spend hours around the garden and in the neighborhood looking for more.

We used to sit down and count them together; she usually won. I think my only purpose was to do something with her because she was beautiful, and unlike other girls, she didn't like to play girly things—she was cool! I liked her, and it was such a pain to leave our summer home that fall.

We had secrets among the children in our neighborhood, such as knowing which flowers had "honey" in them. We knew which flowers around the neighborhood had sweet little parts that we could suck out. We finished them quickly, so every morning we had to check for new ones. We knew which areas had bees and which shortcuts we could take to Migros supermarket without crossing the streets forbidden to us. We never told our parents we went to Migros, but the candy was cheaper there, and we went often.

We never had a worry in the world. If we fell, we knew our body would cover the wound and fix it within days. If we had a problem (whatever problem a child could actually have), our parents fixed it for us. That is, until I nearly died one summer in Caddebostan.

We were playing soccer in the lush green garden of the apartment next to us when our ball landed in the other apartment's garden. None of the kids went to fetch our ball, and they were not saying why. I volunteered, jumped over the fence, and walked to the ball. Then I woke up at home. I was in pain, shouting. There was a bee's nest there that the other kids knew about and didn't tell me. The bees stung me everywhere. I don't remember, but one of my friends came to rescue me, and someone took me to the hospital. Doctors said I was very near death, and even my heart had almost stopped. I was stung everywhere: legs, arms, face, eyelids, even my scalp through my hair. I was in a lot of pain when I came to myself. I spent about two weeks at home until I was strong enough to go out again. I've noticed, though, that bee stings do not hurt me much anymore, and strangely, I'm not afraid of them anymore. I've seen the worst I guess.

Then one summer we moved to Atlanta, Georgia! I was eight years old, and I spent that summer with my mom and dad while they were establishing the US branch of their trading company.

This time, I remember everything—how I couldn't talk to anyone. No one understood me! It was a shock. I wanted to play with the other kids. We had a swimming pool in our complex, and every kid I tried to talk to treated me as if I was stupid. I wasn't; in fact, my IQ is above 140, but I couldn't speak

English. I learned English from the cartoons I watched, which were very limited!

Being alone and having no friends was a very strange experience. I saw other kids play with each other and wanted to play with them, but I didn't know how. I had to find a solution. And I did, when a new kid moved to our complex. I put my cartoon English to work. He was laughing like crazy! It helped, of course, that my mother explained to his mother why I wasn't speaking properly, and we did become friends. I remember John and me playing in the pool, taking turns saying things like, "Me Pac-Man; you ghost," or "Me Jaws; you swim."

Every morning at ten, we had the cartoon hour. A full hour of cartoons! Amazing. Back in Turkey, we had one channel, which was black and white, and we got ten minutes of cartoons on Sundays before the big *Sunday Family Movie*. This was incredible for an eight-year-old, and at eleven, we watched *The Price is Right* with Bob Barker! They were giving away new cars. America was really a land of dreams for an eight-year-old, with Six Flags, Lake Lanier, swimming pools, and tasty food everywhere. I got addicted to the pre-sliced cheddar cheese. We had nothing of that sort in Turkey; all our cheese was white. I ate almost ten of them every day. And Pringles—how strange to have all the chips shaped the same in a tube. Magic!

Every day I was on restriction for at least an hour to read my summer vacation books. We were all assigned books to read during the summer in Turkish elementary school. It was boring, especially when I could hear John playing in the pool—very boring. I had to finish the books quickly, so I found a way. I read the first and last sentence in each paragraph; if it was interesting,

I read the middle. If it was not interesting and not related to the story, such as a long paragraph explaining how the woods looked so nice, I skipped it! I was able to finish all five books in a couple of weeks and explain all the stories to my father, so I got off the hook and went back to playing in the pool.

But then my parents sent me back, all by myself, to Turkey. I remember them handing me over to a nice flight attendant (who really took care of me during the flight) and landing back in Istanbul, which was nothing dreamy compared to my summer in the US.

After two years in Istanbul, this time we all relocated to Atlanta, Georgia, apparently for good. My father had established the US side of his trading company now; and my brother and I went to elementary school there—Rockbridge Elementary. How different it was from Istanbul! My second relocation before I turned ten!

All this time, while having a nice childhood full of summerhouses, swimming, fun, Six Flags, Disneyworld, and so on, my father's new company was not doing so well. That resulted in all of us moving back to Turkey and moving to our better summerhouse. It was my third relocation, and I liked it.

The new summerhouse was in Buyukcekmece, literally the big drawer. It was a pocket of the sea moving inland and creating a nice beach strip. My childhood is full of beautiful memories, mostly of cycling in the strip with my friends and playing basketball.

Close to graduating from high school, I spent a year studying for the university entrance exams in Turkey. They were very difficult, as only a handful of good universities with a limited quota were available. I had always wanted to be an engineer. I was always successful at anything close to math, geometry, and sciences, but I was terrible at history. Well, the top university in Turkey accepted me to their prestigious mechanical engineering program. I was the 337th in the country, but after I started, all hell broke loose!

My father had been working in Krasnoyarsk, Russia, for some time after unsuccessfully forming a computer-services company in Istanbul. He was an architect and accepted a job as a project manager to build a Coca-Cola facility in Russia. As he was not on very good terms with my mom, the distance escalated their issues, and they broke up.

That started an interesting financial situation, where we were living in a huge apartment in the most prestigious part of town in Nisantasi, with my brother attending a private Austrian high school and me attending the most prestigious university in the country, with no money.

I started working by providing private lessons—lucrative work in Turkey if a student was attending my university, which was a stamp of success and technical prowess. Math, physics, and chemistry were my specialties, and I was very good at helping students in high school or helping to prepare them for the university entrance exam. I was able to teach in Turkish and in English, which was necessary for many students in private high schools. I was able to cover my own and some of my family's expenses.

I also started teaching English classes. My accent was obviously American from the time I had spent in the US, and the school was paying dearly for foreign teachers. So, suddenly, I was a Turkish American teaching English. This provided even more for my family and me. However, I remember returning every night at 11 p.m. happy and exhausted. I was even working at a private radio station at seven thirty in the morning. At one point, I was earning more than many engineers would earn with full-time jobs. This was actually necessary to maintain the lifestyle we had.

All this work affected my college success; I graduated with a not-so-impressive GPA. But by that time I had already started to work for an American company—one of the most successful in Turkey and the world. They were anxious for me to graduate so they could justify hiring me as an actual engineer. I graduated with their push, though I was in no hurry. I was trying to graduate as late as I could because in Turkey, after your graduate from college, you need to do military service for up to one and a half years. Obviously, I was in no hurry for that!

I started earning an MBA to keep the military service delayed and continued working in the company. The salary was actually less than what I was earning before. This was a shock, but I was too tired to continue doing everything I had been doing, so I only kept some of the private lessons. By this time, my brother had graduated from high school and started at the same university as me. He was teaching similar private lessons, so I didn't need to work as much.

After three years of hard work in the company and hard work outside, I couldn't postpone the military service anymore. I was about to be thrown out of my MBA program due to attendance, but I couldn't attend and work in the company at the same time. The company came to the rescue and transferred me to Frankfurt, Germany! If I was living outside Turkey, I had time until I was 38 to do my military service. And yes, of all the places I got transferred to Frankfurt, the city I was born in. I spent almost seven years there—some of my happiest times. I had the closest friend group; we called ourselves "Nalos" as in "let's go," and we were always together and took every vacation together.

After Germany, they transferred me to Ukraine with a promotion, and I spent three years in a small town close to Crimea where my ancestors are from. Believe me, life is what you make of it, and those three years included some of my best friends and the best assignment I had had to date. I also worked with the best team in the company—strong Ukrainian women, who are still very successful in the company.

The promised location after Ukraine was Turkey; I had accepted the promotion and assignment with that condition. But then the economic crisis hit, and there were no assignments left in Turkey; people were actually being relocated out of Turkey. I moved to Geneva, Switzerland, and spent one and a half years there in an apartment literally in front of Lac Leman, with incredible views, and I got married!

You may wonder how, through all the relocations and countries, I found my wife. A dear friend introduced us while I was in Ukraine. Believe me, there is no shortage of beautiful women in Ukraine. And I was in and out of some relationships while there. But Deniz, my wife, was the most beautiful thing I'd seen in the world, and she was the most delicate and the loveliest. She certainly had the best character, with a lot of wild parts built in. I called her my pink rose (including the thorns), and I started writing poems for the first time in my life—almost a poem every week, in English and in Turkish.

We spent almost every weekend together in Istanbul. We got married quickly and hurriedly—actually in the middle of a business crisis, so I had to return to work very quickly.

The reason we had to get married quickly was…our green cards! While I was in Ukraine, my brother had accepted a job in Manhattan, New York, and had moved there. After I had moved to Geneva, I won the US green card lottery. I wanted to spend my life with Deniz; therefore, we had to move fast so she could get her green card with me.

Moving fast is not always good. One and a half years later, I'm in my home in the US, alone for the last four months, and getting a divorce. Today, in the evening, I was lost; I was lost for some time, but tonight I had no direction, no future, and no nothing. Nothing made sense anymore; all my plans are obsolete, and everything I lived for has no meaning anymore. What went wrong? What is going on? What kind of a sick joke is this? Is "this" the life we're given? Is this it?

"My God, and please, my God, help me. Help me make sense of it." This was what I was actually praying for. I had tears in my eyes. I was hoping that he really existed and that he would help. And then it happened.

3

THINKING TO MYSELF

To doubt is not sin, but to be contented to remain in doubt when God has provided "many infallible proofs" to cure it, is.

~ Irwin H. Linton

I started thinking very hard on March 31, 2012, at around 9 p.m., with tears in my eyes. It came out of nowhere, but I was almost lecturing myself. Believe it or not, all of the ideas in this book formed in my brain in three hours as if it was a university lecture. I was actually trying to calm myself down. I was angry. I was angry at God. I was angry at how the God I know, the God I'd learned about, could let me suffer so much—how a good God could let bad things happen to good people. How, in general, could bad things even exist?

If you can't believe in God, chances are your God is too small.

~ James Phillips

I kept walking around the house, lecturing myself in my head, and convincing myself. I kept thinking about connections, about God, about good, about free will, about religion, about what I should do, about what everyone should do, and about what everyone should know and why they don't know it. I was surprised, but I didn't stop; I kept on. This was a first for me; it had never happened before. I always been thoughtful and thought hard about decisions, but I had never done it so intensely! I was pacing through the apartment forming ideas and linking them to each other. At times, I felt very strange, but it was good because it was making sense. It was as if someone else was lecturing me. I was asking, praying, and pleading to God to help me make sense, and suddenly it was making sense. I was making sense and finally connecting everything.

Please believe me that I wasn't on drugs; I don't take drugs except from a doctor. I don't even drink much alcohol and hadn't even had a beer for weeks. I wasn't high on anything, but euphoria took over me. It was like a connect-the-dots picture. Suddenly I was seeing the picture, and I was explaining it to myself!

Every idea in this book was coming to me almost already prepared. I don't believe God talks to us, and I don't believe it was directly from him. But I do believe at this point in my life that all my experiences, beliefs, thoughts, disbeliefs, sorrows, and anger were connecting with a brief intelligent brilliance, which is part of God's will. And it was pouring out. It was magical.

That night I quit smoking, and I will explain why in the following chapters. That night I forgave my father, and I will explain that as well. My new life started that night. I wrote the introduction and the outlines of the chapters you are reading now. I wrote down all the points for the next chapters because I was worried I would forget everything in the morning. I didn't sleep anyway until early morning, and I didn't forget anything.

The next chapters have all the ideas from that night and a few additions I added later, such as the quotations, verses from sacred texts, and some of my experiences that related to the ideas in the chapter. In essence, I did not change the sequence nor the ideas and examples that I had dictated to myself that night.

4

CULTURE

What you don't understand is that it is possible to be an atheist, it is possible not to know if God exists or why He should, and yet to believe that man does not live in a state of nature but in history, and that history as we know it now began with Christ, it was founded by Him on the Gospels.

~ Boris Pasternak

We are what we are thanks to the cultures we grew up in. Culture is actually an agri "cultur" al term. Its etymology suggests that it comes from the verb cultivate, meaning to grow or to provide for. For example, a plant grows in a culture, and the culture provides the seed everything it needs to become more than a seed. Everything the plant grows into comes from the culture except the initial design that is in the seed.

The initial design that is in the seed is similar to our initial design given to us by God. This we cannot change; it governs how we're going to grow and develop. On the other hand, everything else, such as our physical presence and our bodies build from the physical things we eat, which the "cultures" we're in provide.

On a more spiritual sense, on top of our initial design (a human being with free will designed by God), everything else is provided by the culture we live in. All our beliefs, the way we dress, the way we behave, the way we live, the way we work, the way we take and give education, our language, our religion, and even our likes and dislikes came from the culture of the societies we grew up in.

I had the rare chance to grow up in different cultures. With this opportunity, I am about 50 percent Turkish, 25 percent German, 10 percent Ukrainian, 5 percent Swiss, and 10 percent American so far. And this changes as I adapt and learn more and more in the US. There are definitely commonalities between these cultures and definitely many contradictions. It is interesting to feel these contradictions inside me and have the opportunity to choose which one fits my conscience.

Being aware of our initial designs (human beings with free will given to us by God) and knowing that everything else comes from the cultures we're in are important distinctions from what we live by today. Not being aware about the process of why we feel or think the way we do is a mistake none of us should make. I constantly feel strange contradictions, as my American, German, Turkish, etc. sides contradict each other. You may not feel the same contradictions with the integrity of one culture providing you with one path. Still, remember that you only share one design with every other human being on this planet—the one design that God created for us. All the other beliefs are results of the culture we grew up in and may be right or wrong! And in many cases, such as our modern eating habits, subtle racist thoughts, or feelings of unjustified superiority against other groups or nations are actually wrong.

5

UNIVERSAL DESIGN

An atheist is a man who believes himself an accident.

~ Francis Thompson

We are the only creation with free will. Nothing else around us has free will. That is an amazing concept. God designs animals as well. But animals cannot decide to do anything they do not have designs to do. The same goes for plants and everything living or not living around us. They have specific purposes and paths they must follow. They can decide to go left or right, but their designs will dictate their decisions. For example, a lioness will not decide to avoid eating a deer because it's too cute. If it is hungry, the deer is dinner.

Have we not all one Father? Has not one God created us? Why then are we faithless to one another, profaning the covenant of our fathers?

Malachi 2:10

We are the only creation that can decide, and we can even decide out of our design. If you believe we have a design not to eat meat for example, humans had already decided thousands of years ago that they were going to eat meat. Or if you believe the opposite, that we have a design to eat meat, millions today have decided they are vegetarians and will never eat meat. However you look at it, we humans are given free will to choose what we do, "even if" it is against our design.

6

GODLY FREE WILL

During the crusades all were religious mad, and now all are mad for want of it.

~ Captain J. G. Stedman

We share the power of free will with only one more being: the creator himself, who provided us with such power. It was his free will to give us somewhat limited free will. With his gift, we can even decide things outside our original design, and it is important to know that we can do this because not everything we decide to do is right.

Then God said, "Let Us make man in Our image, according to Our likeness; let them have dominion over the fish of the sea, over the birds of the air, and over the cattle, over all the earth and over every creeping thing that creeps on the earth."

Genesis 1:26

I can, and you can choose to do good, bad, charity, or evil with our power and our money. We can easily choose to do the wrong thing. Wrong may be defined by the culture we grew up in, but we also have a tool that points us always in the right direction: our conscience.

7

GODLY CONSCIENCE

There is no being eloquent for atheism. In that exhausted receiver the mind cannot use its wings,- the clearest proof that it is out of its element.

~ Hare

Of course, God provided a fail-safe mechanism for our free will. How can I know what is right or wrong if I grew up in different cultures, with different rights and wrongs? Well, as mentioned above, that fail-safe mechanism is my conscience. For every cultural aspect, my conscience double-checks and approves what is right.

Then Paul, looking earnestly at the council, said, "Men and brethren, I have lived in all good conscience before God until this day."

Acts 23:1

This being so, I myself always strive to have a conscience without offense toward God and men.

Acts 24:16

...who show the work of the law written in their hearts, their conscience also bearing witness, and between themselves their thoughts accusing or else excusing them...

Romans 2:15

Even in cultures that may have different views on what is right and wrong, many people who grow up in the same culture see issues with their own culture and push to move their culture to the universal right. For example, even in ancient cultures that saw human sacrifice as normal, many people in that same culture objected to this and, whatever the consequence, advocated to stop such a practice.

In many of our religions, the same advocation shows up, substituting and correcting such practices with acceptable, "right" alternatives.

For our boasting is this: the testimony of our conscience that we conducted ourselves in the world in simplicity and godly sincerity, not with fleshly wisdom but by the grace of God, and more abundantly toward you.

2 Corinthians 1:12

But we have renounced the hidden things of shame, not walking in craftiness nor handling the word of God deceitfully, but by manifestation of the truth commending ourselves to every man's conscience in the sight of God.

2 Corinthians 4:2

Knowing, therefore, the terror of the Lord, we persuade men; but we are well known to God, and I also trust are well known in your consciences.

2 Corinthians 5:11

Now the purpose of the commandment is love from a pure heart, from a good conscience, and from sincere faith…

1 Timothy 1:5

…having faith and a good conscience, which some having rejected, concerning the faith have suffered shipwreck…

1 Timothy 1:19

…holding the mystery of the faith with a pure conscience.

1 Timothy 3:9

...speaking lies in hypocrisy, having their own conscience seared with a hot iron...

1 Timothy 4:2

Some of our feelings, decisions, and ways of life come from our cultures, which are *not* godly and are a complete invention of our ancestors. This is an important revelation to keep in mind throughout this book. The only fail-safe mechanism is your own conscience, which is Godly or given by God. If something doesn't seem right, it probably isn't—whatever your customs, education, and normal way of life may otherwise suggest.

For God knows that in the day you eat of it your eyes will be opened, and you will be like God, knowing good and evil.

Genesis 3:5

Then the Lord God said, "Behold, the man has become like one of Us, to know good and evil. And now, lest he put out his hand and take also of the tree of life, and eat, and live forever..."

Genesis 3:22

8

DO YOU BELIEVE IN GOD?

No man will say, "There is no God" 'till he is so hardened in sin that it has become his interest that there should be none to call him to account.

~ Mathew Henry

I'm sorry, but many devoted, religious people are atheists. So was I until my revelation, and you might be, too, until now. Some of our fellow humans clearly believe he doesn't exist, and it is their free will to think and believe this way. The real issue is with people who say they believe in God. They may have chosen a religion or been handed one by the cultures they grew up in. Many people that believe in God actually do *not* believe in him.

And he believed the Lord, and he counted it to him as righteousness.

Genesis 15:6

Let me explain this hidden atheism more clearly. If someone believes in God truly and fully, without any doubt in his or her mind, there's no chance ever that this person will do anything wrong or unjust.

The belief in God comes with a belief that he is omnipotent, is omnipresent, sees everything that we do, knows everything that we think, and is ever powerful. He has made it clear that there are consequences to our actions in the afterlife, which many religions detail.

So, if almost all people in the major parts of our societies believe in God, in his qualifications, and that there will be consequences to their actions, how is it possible that many people are still committing wrong, evil acts?

A disbelief in God does not result in a belief in nothing; disbelief in God usually results in a belief in anything.

~Arthur Lynch

It is impossible to truly believe in God and at the same time do something wrong—even if it's a small trick in your business that provides you more money, even if it's a small act at school against another child, even if it's calling somebody by a bad name, or talking bad about people behind their backs. If you truly believe in God, you must be paranoid about doing something wrong.

Atheism is rather in the life than in the heart of man.

~ Francis Bacon

He sees everything you do and knows everything you think. How is it not possible to become paranoid about doing something wrong? When these words were coming out of my mouth, I was shocked! I knew I would never be able to do anything wrong knowingly. It is now impossible.

And if you truly believe in God, and if you truly understand my message, it is now impossible for you too. You cannot knowingly do anything wrong in front of your creator, the one God you owe everything to, the one being who loves you eternally, and the one who is seeing your actions, feeling your feelings, and knowing your thoughts.

"You are My witnesses," says the Lord,
"And My servant whom I have chosen,
That you may know and believe Me,
And understand that I am He.
Before Me there was no God formed,
Nor shall there be after Me."

Isaiah 43:10

I will clarify what is a wrong act in general terms, and it may be very different to what you think it is due to the culture you grew up in.

9

GOD WILL FORGIVE ME!

Atheism is the result of ignorance and pride; of strong sense and feeble reasons; of good eating and ill-living. It is the plague of society, the corrupter of manners, and the underminer of property.

~ Jeremy Collier

Yes, God is forgiving. Almost every religion clarifies this. God will forgive us for the sins we commit unknowingly. For example, people with mental disabilities are not going to be judged according to many religions. Also in many religions, you may ask for forgiveness, and he may forgive you.

It is important to connect God's forgiveness to the fact that he's the universal, eternal, and ultimate symbol of justice. God is just in every religion, and he sides with and protects the people who are right. In other words, God is ultimately just.

What does "God is just" mean? This means that in any conflict, God knows who is right and who is wrong. Your conscience also knows and tries to help you in the right direction. Cultural elements or earthly favors and pleasures may push you in the wrong direction; however, even if you decide to do something wrong with your free will, *you will know that it is wrong*. And while doing something wrong, the small (even if infinitesimal) doubt that God exists, the smallest belief of atheism, and the small chance that you think you can get away with it will ease your pain of doing the wrong thing. And you will focus on the earthly pleasure, the money, or whatever gain you expect from your wrongdoing.

God knows you did something wrong, and he will forgive you if the wrong was about him. What does this mean? If the wrong you did was solely about God, something only between him and you, God is all forgiving and may forgive you. For example, if, according to your religion, you needed to fast at a specific time but you didn't for whatever reason, as long as this caused no harm to anyone else and was between God and you, he may forgive you.

Let's assume you did something wrong against a fellow human being, such as cheated him out of money, charged him more than you should have, told a lie that hurt him, stole from him, or did something worse, would God forgive you? No!

These wrongdoings are even worse if they are against many people. For example, if a politician uses his status and power to gain material favors, he is effectively stealing from his whole nation. Will God forgive him? No! Even worse is a politician that passes legislature risking his nation's health because some giant company pushes a dangerous chemical as safe. How can God forgive such a huge sin when this wrongdoing will affect millions of people? How God-believing politicians can do many of the things they do today baffles me, unless they are secretly atheists. And, as I said, many seemingly religious people actually are.

God will not forgive you for the wrong things you knowingly do to another one of his creations, whether it's a human being, an animal, a plant, or the earth itself, for a very simple reason. Forgiving you would not be "just" to the other creation, and God is ultimately just. He will not forgive you. The only person who can forgive you is the person you did the wrong to.

10

THE ULTIMATE DECISION

An atheist is one who hopes the Lord will do nothing to disturb his disbelief.

~ Franklin P. Jones

What is a decision? A decision is eliminating all the other opportunities, paths, options, and chances and choosing one. In our lives, unfortunately, we're no longer making decisions. We're forgetting what a decision is. A decision is ultimate. You decide and then you do; there's no turning back, no reconsideration, and no fallback option. In our modern society, we've created so many chances for us to change our decisions that we no longer make decisions. Instead, we show a soft "want." For example, we buy and return. We say, "I decided to go hunting this weekend" while actually meaning "I want to go hunting this weekend if it doesn't rain." It's not really a decision;

it's a preference! "I decided to get married with you" is actually, "I want to get married with you, and continue until I am one day dissatisfied."

A decision is and should be a firm path, where all the other paths are eliminated whatever the consequence. We see these indecision preferences many times in challenges about ourselves. For example, "I've decided to lose weight" now means, "I'm going to try to lose weight until it becomes too difficult, and then I will stop." "I've decided to quit smoking" means "I will try to quit smoking now; I hope I really can." There's no hope in a decision. There's no other option anymore in a decision. You decide, and then you do it. Otherwise, let's all stop using this word altogether.

Asking for forgiveness is the ultimate decision. We need to be very careful, because we cannot ask anyone, let alone God, for forgiveness twice!

> *Judge not, and you shall not be judged. Condemn not, and you shall not be condemned. Forgive, and you will be forgiven.*
>
> Luke 6:37

There's a joke about a rich guy who had just bought a nice sports car. While driving it for the first time, a truck hit him from behind. There was not much damage, and the truck driver said he was really sorry. He was poor and asked for forgiveness. The rich guy, being a nice guy, forgave him. At the next red light, the same truck driver strongly hit the new sports car again, causing more damage. The truck driver hung out of his truck and shouted, "It's me. It's me; carry on!"

Asking for forgiveness means that you will not knowingly make the same mistake again. You're making a decision—a real decision—not the "want" kind, and you're asking for an acceptance of this decision by the person you're pleading forgiveness from. You're asking the person to free you from the consequences of your first mistake on the premise that you will not knowingly do it again.

The person you're asking forgiveness from judges your sincerity and your decision's strength and may choose to forgive you or not with his or her free will. Sometimes you may try to balance your wrongdoing by doing something right to the person to move his choice in your favor, such as offering compensation.

Asking for forgiveness from God is the same, except he does not need your compensation; he only needs your firm decision that you will never make the same mistake again. You cannot ask for forgiveness for the same mistake again and again; that's not asking for forgiveness. That is subtle atheism— thinking God has to grant you forgiveness. He does not have to grant you anything.

Whatever religion you believe or do not believe in, please keep in mind two important points:

- *God will not forgive you for your wrongdoing to another one of his creations.*
- *God does not have to grant you forgiveness again and again.*

11

SINS THAT CAN'T BE FORGIVEN

If you don't believe in God, all you have to believe in is decency. Decency is very good. Better decent than indecent. But I don't think it's enough.

~ Harold Macmillan

We mentioned wrongdoings about something that was strictly between you and God, which he can forgive once. We also mentioned wrongdoings to other humans, which the other humans can forgive you for so you won't suffer the consequences. But, what if you did something wrong to another one of God's creations?

Humans are the only creation of God that has free will and, therefore, a choice to forgive or not. An animal does not have a free will, and it is still God's creation. Our duty is to benefit from God's creations and *not* do anything wrong to them because they cannot forgive us, and it would be unjust for God to forgive us regarding this.

For example, some children in poor societies torture street animals, cats, and dogs. They tie ropes around them, hurt them, blind them, and even kill them. This is clearly wrong. A normal conscience will tell them those acts are wrong and sinful. The animals they torture do not have free wills, so even if they nurse them back to health and give them plenty of food, the animals are in no position to understand fully what is going on. Consequently, they are in no position to forgive the wrongdoings.

Therefore, this type of sinful wrongdoing would go unforgiven, and a just God would not forgive you; otherwise, it would be injustice to the other creations. Benefitting from God's other creations brings with it tremendous responsibility to not do anything wrong to these creations. For example, we cannot treat animals with cruelty even if they are in our food chain; we must treat them humanely. And if you're buying what I call "cruelty meat," you may be part of this sin. The same is true for plants, wild animals, and the earth itself. They are all God's creations, and all deserve respectful treatment. Our duty is to protect them while benefitting from them; otherwise, we will not receive forgiveness for our wrongdoings.

Wrongdoing to the earth has an extra unforgivable sin associated with it. Earth is not just personally ours; all people, animals, plants, and creations of God share it. Hurting the earth is sin toward every human and creature now and in the future. How can people risk such a sin, knowing it is unforgivable, unless they are secret atheists?

12

FORGIVE YOURSELF

Atheist's don't exist. If you ask anyone why they are an atheist they will proceed to explain their religion of non belief.

~ Monksarnn

So far, I've tried to clarify that God may forgive us for the things between him and us personally. It would be unjust for him to forgive us for the things between us and his other creations. The interesting twist here is that we personally are also one of his creations.

I've done many bad things to myself. I'm overweight, I don't work out, and I smoke. I'm not looking after my body, which is a creation of God and one that only I am fully responsible for. "I" am actually doing wrong things to one of God's creations, my body, and myself!

And whenever you stand praying, if you have anything against anyone, forgive him, that your Father in heaven may also forgive you your trespasses.

Mark 11:25

But if you do not forgive, neither will your Father in heaven forgive your trespasses.

Mark 11:26

When I uttered these words that night, I quit smoking. It was sudden, but just saying these words, I knew I couldn't smoke anymore! It was a mistake, a sin I committed again and again. Many times, I had decided to quit, but never in the true sense, more of the "want" kind. I tried all the techniques to quit, but only this revelation made me truly decide to quit. And, as we discussed earlier, a true decision is ultimate. My decision was so joyful; I cannot even try to explain it to you. Just knowing I would never smoke again was so overwhelmingly beautiful.

And I knew it was not only about smoking. Realizing that I would look after myself properly now and forever was an amazing feeling. I sincerely hope the thought process and the facts I lay out in front of you will help you achieve the same and that you will join me in this revelation and joy.

I forgive myself, in the true sense of the word.
I forgive myself, "deciding" that I will not make
the same mistakes again.

Simple and easy it seems,
why has it been so difficult before?

13

EASIEST THINGS ARE THE MOST DIFFICULT

The only atheism is the denial of truth.

~Arthur Lynch

There's not a force in this world that can make you do something you don't want.

Do you believe the above fact? It was a revelation to me that night that everything I was doing was under my control. Amazing! This gives me so much power. Maybe you don't believe me. Perhaps you feel you need to do things because you have to, because your boss tells you to, or because your wife or husband tells you to.

Wrong. You never do anything without your own conscious decision. Your mind constantly weighs—perhaps unconsciously—every possibility. Your mind has the ultimate job of looking after your body and spiritually looking after your mind. And these may be contradicting sometimes. If you let your mind do its job on autopilot, it will choose the most beneficial path for your mind and/or your body. If no path is beneficial, it will choose the least painful and/or least damaging path. And, it will react in the ultimate conservationist fashion, trying to achieve the best result with the least energy/effort spent.

If your boss tells you to do something that you don't want to do, your mind will weigh the energy/effort needed to do it versus the benefit/damage you may get from not doing it. You will feel, "Ah, I have to do it because my boss told me to," but you are actually deciding to do it! The real result your mind achieves is, "I decide to do this thing that I don't want to do because not doing it will damage me/my career/my job/my financial situation in this XYZ way." Again, a clear distinction of want and decide but on the other side of the coin.

Being aware of this powerful fact really helped me that night. I felt back in control. I actually realized that I was never *not* in control. Everything I do, I decided. It dawned on me that if it is my decision to do it anyway, then it deserves my best. I will do my best on everything I do, or I will decide not to do it. There's no adequate doing, getting by, or so-so result that I want to achieve. Either I want to give "my all" to "my" decision, or I might as well not do it at all.

14

FORGIVE OTHERS

No one can be an unbeliever nowadays. The Christian Apologists have left one nothing to disbelieve.

~ Hector Hugh Munro

After I quit smoking that night, I was contemplating and thinking about how we want to be like God. In many of our religions, God has created us in his image, meaning he has created us similar to himself like none of his other creations. I believe this means that, like him, we have free will that he has given us. Our ultimate happiness lies in trying to be like him, trying to be close to him.

So, if our happiness is linked to being like God, what are some of God's traits?

God is:

- Right
- Just
- Forgiving
- Creative

Except for creativity, we've explored his rightness, justness, and forgiveness. Forgiving myself was a great revelation for me that night. It was a promise to myself to accept my apologies, and it was a decision, a true decision, to never make the same mistakes again—just as a real request for forgiveness should be.

I noticed we might forgive without being asked. I noticed that God would forgive us for the things between him and us, even if we didn't ask him to, because he's very forgiving. And we are happier when we are closer to him, more like him. However, I was missing something.

I was missing forgiving people who don't or can't ask for forgiveness. I noticed I was angry when I started thinking. I was angry at God because I didn't understand many of the things I had written, and I was angry at my wife for letting me down. I noticed another huge anger buried deep inside of me that had been making me an unhappy man for so long.

And forgive us our debts, As we forgive our debtors.

Matthew 6:12

For if you forgive men their trespasses [mistakes], your heavenly Father will also forgive you.

Matthew 6:14

But if you do not forgive men their trespasses [mistakes], neither will your Father forgive your trespasses [mistakes].

Matthew 6:15

I was angry at my dad. I knew I had been angry at him all my life, and he just passed away this Christmas. I was angry at him because he no longer had the chance to make things right! He blew it. He could have apologized to me for letting me down and for not being there when I needed him physically, spiritually, and financially. I loved my dad, but I was very angry because he had not done the right thing according to me. I realized that there was nothing I could do anymore about him. He passed away, which was making me even angrier.

I had felt this anger all my life, and I realized there was a reason why God was forgiving. He was forgiving because he had created us; he knew exactly what he had created. We have free will, and we will make mistakes. Sometimes knowingly and sometimes unknowingly, we will do the wrong things. The ones damaged by these mistakes have two paths to take, and even this involves our free will. We can decide to forgive the person who did a wrong thing toward us, or we can decide not to forgive the person and see that he or she suffers the consequence in the afterlife.

God is great to have given us free will. Free will opens us to make mistakes, and the mistakes have consequences to other humans. When this happens, God is showing us what to do if we can find it in ourselves. We would be happier if we were like God; in fact, all our life we strive to be like him, closer to him. We can never be exactly him, or we can never be another God, though we strive to be like him. And he shows us the way.

- Be forgiving

This doesn't mean you have to forgive someone again and again, but forgiving frees you of negative feelings and helps you become closer to God, more like him as he is also forgiving.

Then Peter came to Him and said, "Lord, how often shall my brother sin against me, and I forgive him? Up to seven times?"

Matthew 18:21

So My heavenly Father also will do to you if each of you, from his heart, does not forgive his brother his trespasses [mistakes].

Matthew 18:35

As I was still thinking about how forgiving is godly, I suddenly noticed that I had just now forgiven my father. I didn't forget what happened, and I still resent his decisions, but I don't want him to suffer because I don't forgive him. I loved him.

15

CREATE LIKE GOD

Among the repulsions of atheism for me has been its drastic uninterestingness as an intellectual position. Where was the ingenuity, the ambiguity, the humanity (in the Harvard sense) of saying that the universe just happened to happen and that when we're dead we're dead?

~ John Updike

God is the creator; he can decide and make anything happen. He can create material from nothing. Creating from nothing is a godly act. Can we, mere humans create from nothing? According to my physics teacher, we can't.

Yes, we can create from nothing, but we cannot create materials from nothing. We can create only one thing from nothing—ideas.

Creating an idea is the closest we can get to godly creation. If it's an original idea, it literally did not exist before we shaped it in our minds. This is one of the gifts God gave us: creativity!

Truly, truly, I say to you, whoever believes in me will also do the works that I do; and greater works than these will he do, because I am going to the Father.

John 14:12

Some animals have limited creativity, such as using tools and teaching their offspring how to use them. But we have a tremendous ability to create ideas. We can think, analyze, and come up with ideas and solutions that never existed before—purely original innovations.

It's tremendously rewarding to come up with an innovative idea or an original solution to a complex problem. It feels great because it is a godly act. It is another way for us to be like God and to be closer to him, which is what he wants. He created us in his image! When we do things like him, we enjoy them, and we're happy.

I decided that night how grateful I was to God, how happy I was that I could think, and that I could think of these things. Whether original or not, I was doing something he wanted me to do. My gratefulness exploded in such a way that I became happier and happier the more I thought about these concepts.

16

WANT FOR THE RIGHT REASONS

I had convinced myself that God wants us to be happy, and he would give us everything we need or want to be happy. I was still perplexed why many bad things were happening to good people. And for this, I didn't have an answer. My only thoughts were that God sees the full picture and knows much more than us. Therefore, like many things about God, those reasons are outside our comprehension.

Therefore I tell you, whatever you ask in prayer, believe that you have received it, and it will be yours.

Mark 11:24

Still, I was convinced that he would give us what we wanted. While I was thinking about this, my mind started to circle around why we want things.

For everyone who asks receives, and the one who seeks finds, and to the one who knocks it will be opened.

Matthew 7:8

Why do we want things? I want a faster computer. Why? It annoys me when I have to wait a few seconds for a program to open; it would be nice if it took less time. In order to add speed to my computer, I would need more money. Therefore, I want more money. Ok, we have clarified why I want money.

And whatever you ask in prayer, you will receive, if you have faith.

Matthew 21:22

I'm sorry, but I don't think a few seconds on my computer is on God's priority list. I don't know if he has a priority list, but I actually think he wouldn't give me more money because I want it for such a stupid reason.

Then it occurred to me that God would provide for me if my reasons were to do godly tasks. I wouldn't get anything if my reasons were purely selfish. Why should I? If I asked for something from God to do good things for my family, my community, the nation, the country, or myself, why wouldn't he provide what I asked for? If I asked for something to do godly acts for righteousness, justice, forgiveness, or creativity, why wouldn't he provide what I asked for?

I understand that I am his tool; if I'm not going to do his bidding, there's no reason for him to especially provide for me. I can do a lot of things. I have my free will and equal opportunities with everyone, but if I'm asking for something special from him, it needs to be for the things he wants me to do.

17

WANT AND YOU SHALL RECEIVE, BUT WHEN?

The three great apostles of practical atheism, that make converts without persecuting, and retain them without preaching, are wealth, health and power.

~ C.C. Colton

If there is something you want from God, as long as you take action to achieve it and the reasons you want it are in line with what he wants you to do, you will receive it.

Be patient, therefore, brothers, until the coming of the Lord. See how the farmer waits for the precious fruit of the earth, being patient about it, until it receives the early and the late rains.

James 5:7

I wanted a lot of things from my life. A job I had wanted before joining my current company included heavy traveling. I didn't get that job, and I remember talking with friends about how I would have enjoyed traveling and how it would have made me a more open and knowledgeable person. Three years later, I moved into a role that allowed me to travel 75 percent of the time for two years. I loved it and thanked God for it. Then I remembered that I had asked for that. I went after a role in the company where I could form my own team and train and develop the team members, but I didn't get it. I was angry; I thought it was unfair they chose a more experienced person because I felt I could do it. Two years later, I was in Ukraine with a technician team of 120 people who I taught and grew almost ten of them to managers. I also organized two departments. It was the best assignment of my life, and I thanked God. Ever since we attended elementary school in the US, my brother and I wanted to live there. It is amazing that we're both here now, that I won the lottery for it, and that he came here by a freak coincidence! Nothing happened when I wanted it, but eventually they did.

For everything there is a season,
and a time for every matter under heaven:
a time to be born, and a time to die;
a time to plant, and a time to pluck up what is planted;
a time to kill, and a time to heal;
a time to break down, and a time to build up;
a time to weep, and a time to laugh;
a time to mourn, and a time to dance. . . .

Ecclesiastes 3:1–4

God knows the reasons we don't understand why bad things happen to good people. He also knows when to give us what we want, but it is not always when we want it. He has good reasons for his timing, and sometimes he uses his timing to teach us lessons or for other purposes. For example, the fact that I had won the green card lottery expedited my decision to get married and saved my wife and me a lot of time.

Comparing this life to the afterlife is an interesting difference. In the afterlife, (in heaven) according to many religions, we will get whatever we want, whenever we want it. That is definitely not true in this life, where we're not sure if or when we will get what we want.

I compare this with police and handguns. A person in the US can own a gun as a constitutional right. There are, however, regulations around gun ownership in many states that often include waiting periods. The registration and regulations link a person to a gun, ensuring that the gun is traceable to that person. Therefore, the person is much less likely to use the gun for crime, and the waiting period discourages the person from using it to commit a crime out of anger. During this waiting period, the person would presumably come to his or her senses. Also, many states have additional checks to ensure the person is of sound personality, so there is acceptable proof that the gun will not be used for any wrongdoing.

I felt this was somewhat similar to getting what you asked for. I think there needs to be considerable proof that your wants are consistent and for the good of your family, your community, and yourself—not from emotions.

Well, where are the police in this picture? A police officer can get a gun without restrictions and waiting periods. Why is that so? He has proven throughout his training and acceptance to the force that his intentions are good with regards to the gun he needs. I compared that to the unknown amount of time we need to wait to achieve our goals, dreams, and passions. Only after we've proven to God that our intentions are good—and we've proven that we're going to use what we receive for the well-being of all things created—will we receive it in this life. Many religions state that in afterlife we will get whatever we want, whenever we want it because we will have already passed the test and made it to heaven.

18

CLOSER TO GOD

He who never thirsts for God here, will thirst for Him before he has been dead a minute.

~ B. North

I personally do not believe there's a comparable life after death. This doesn't mean I don't believe in afterlife, heaven, and hell. I do believe in them; I just don't believe they will be as many religions describe them. Trying to describe heaven and hell in this life, with our languages, is like trying to explain a 4-D object. We can conceptualize it but never fully explain it. We add comparisons and concepts of 3-D but cannot visualize it in our minds. I feel that all our lives we would like to be like God and be closer to God. I imagine heaven as a place where God is there—like the sun—and we're around him. The people who were better in this life would be just a little bit closer to him than people who have not been so good. People who have been bad would be further in the back. Imagine what kind of pain and suffering it would be to be in the back, that you're even if a little bit further from the one, great God, your creator, and your sole aspiration. You lived a whole life that was given to you by him, and now you're not as close to him as you could have been because of how you spent your life. How much happier you would be if you were a little bit closer to him, as this is the only criteria in the afterlife, how close you are to God.

Heaven is often associated with this world's pleasures, but the only pleasure I would seek is to be closer to God. I wouldn't think of having any use of worldly things.

Hell is associated with suffering, pain, and fire—pain symbols from this world. Being further away from God would be the ultimate suffering, I can't think of anything more painful than knowing God might love people in front of me more than he loves me. He created me, and the people in front of me satisfied him more than I did. And in the afterlife, I would no longer have the chance to correct my mistakes. I'd be eternally set in that position, close to God but not as close as I could have been. What more suffering do I need? I don't need fire...

AFTERWORD

I wrote this part of the book a few weeks after my revelation night. I discuss a few things here that I remember thinking about, but I can no longer exactly place them in the flow. I don't want to add them arbitrarily, as I'd like to keep the above chapters in the order that I wrote them that night. I've since extended those chapters, but I kept the flow untouched.

The first thing I remembered thinking about (that I didn't find in my notes) was a discussion with myself about how much quicker it would be to achieve goals if people didn't believe in God. People can disrupt God's timing with their free wills. They can use free will to steal from others, cheat others into paying more, cheat in the production of goods (even foods), and replace genuine products with cheaper copies because it brings better profits!

Is an auto salesperson cheating a buyer when he sells a car for more than it's worth? This same salesperson might go to church on Sunday and pray to a God he secretly hopes doesn't exist. He's not even aware that he's a secret atheist, but he is. Think about the executive who replaces a natural ingredient in the food his company produces with an artificial and harmful ingredient because it's cheaper or because it makes people eat more—resulting in bigger profits. I bet that executive is a devout, religious, well-respected individual, perhaps even donating some of these "cheating" profits to charity! If God exists, he's going to look at this executive's sins and won't forgive him because the sins are against other creations.

I'm not blaming anybody; I'm blaming everybody—including myself—for not being paranoid about doing the right thing. All I ask is that you truly, fully believe God exists, and believe that he knows what you're doing. Then you just can't do the wrong thing. With this true belief, link what you desire in this life to the things he desires for his creations. If you want to be famous, for example, know in your mind, decide, and commit that you will use your fame for the good of other people, animals, plants, and the earth. When you prove that your intentions are in line with God's intentions, he will provide, and you will receive.

The trigger of this book was my fathers passing away and the issues we were having with my wife. The ideas in this book, the ideas of that night; helped me forgive my father, for the first and last time in my life. After a few weeks I wrote the chapters we were also able to come to a better understanding with my wife, and we're working towards a future that we would both be happy together. I don't know the future yet, what I know is that God wants me and everyone to be happy, and he will make it happen.

THE RECIPE

1. Truly, fully, genuinely <u>believe that God exists</u> and knows everything you are doing and thinking.

2. Be aware that almost all your beliefs today result from the culture, society, family, school, and country you grew up in and <u>may be right as well as wrong</u>.

3. Be aware that you are <u>the only creation with free will</u>, and no one can make you do anything unless it's your choosing.

4. Get to know your <u>conscience</u>, practice using it, and ask questions to it. Get your conscience to decide. You will know the right thing to do.

5. A decision is <u>the ultimate end to other options</u>. Don't take it lightly; decide only when you're ready, and fully follow through with your decision.

6. Asking for forgiveness is a big decision of <u>committing to never doing the same mistake again</u>.

7. Be aware of <u>sins that God cannot forgive</u>: any wrongdoing toward any one of God's other creations.

8. <u>Ask for forgiveness</u> from the people you may have wronged, and try to get forgiveness from them.

9. Do your best to compensate for the sins you may have committed against <u>creations that cannot forgive you</u>, such as the earth, animals, and plants.

10. Forgive <u>others.</u>

11. Forgive <u>yourself.</u>

12. Create like God, <u>create ideas</u>, and leave anything and everything you touch in significantly better shape than before.

13. Desire and want big things <u>for the right reasons and</u> for your own personal well-being as well as the well-being and benefit of other creations.

14. Don't get hung up on when your desires will materialize; as you <u>prove your intentions to God</u>, he knows the best timing.

AUTHOR BIOGRAPHY

Michael User is an executive who has been interested in philosophy all his life. He has joined many philosophy-focused organizations in different parts of the world. He was born in Frankfurt am Main, Germany, in 1974 and spent his childhood in Istanbul, Turkey, and Atlanta, Georgia. He has lived in Germany, Ukraine, and Switzerland and currently resides in Danbury, Connecticut, with his wife and their cat.

www.ingramcontent.com/pod-product-compliance
Lightning Source LLC
Chambersburg PA
CBHW020517030426
42337CB00011B/437